John William Lloyd

Wind-harp Songs

John William Lloyd

Wind-harp Songs

ISBN/EAN: 9783744766920

Printed in Europe, USA, Canada, Australia, Japan

Cover: Foto ©Thomas Meinert / pixelio.de

More available books at **www.hansebooks.com**

WIND-HARP SONGS

BY

J. WILLIAM LLOYD

The poets are thus liberating gods. The ancient British bards had for the title of their order, "Those who are free throughout the world." They are free, and they make free. — EMERSON, *The Poet*.

The poet has a new thought; he has a whole new experience to unfold; he will tell us how it was with him, and all men will be the richer in his fortune.
— IBID.

The poet also resigns himself to his mood.
— IBID.

AUTHOR'S EDITION

BUFFALO
THE PETER PAUL BOOK COMPANY
1895

COPYRIGHT, 1895,
BY J. WILLIAM LLOYD.

PRINTED AND BOUND BY
THE PETER PAUL BOOK COMPANY,
BUFFALO, N. Y.

*DEDICATED TO
THE
FREE SPIRIT*

FORE WORD

Songs of my winged-thoughts, of life, nature, love, and liberty; composed not for the public, but my own pleasure,—on the plains, in the forest, in the wake of the plow, on horseback, on the crowded street, by the bedside of death, in the storm, the silence of midnight, and when the face of the God of Morning blushed through the golden tresses of Dawn.

The fire burned within, the flames sang, and the free winds fanned them to music.

From the harp of fire, with the wind's touch, came these, and the writing of them was my joy and easement.

I have no apology.

Poetry is not to be excused. Like music it is a glory or an offence.

CONTENTS.

	PAGE
Dedication	3
Fore Word	5
Proem	11
The Wind-Harp Song . . .	13
The Wish of Womanhood . .	17
In Touch	17
Aphorism: Woman	17
My Dead	18
The Soul Supreme	20
Cupid	21
Freedom	21
I Am Glad—Are Not You? . .	22
Only a Memory	23
My Lady Gentle Wonderful . .	24
The Greek Anthology . . .	25
True Love	26
Death's Word	27
Mother	28
Emily Dickenson	31
Remember	32
The Smell of Rain-Wet Earth .	33
The Moon-Shark	33
Mount Walt Whitman . . .	34
Robert Bloomfield . . .	36
Aztec of the Air . . .	36
Poetry	37
The Day-Birth	38
The White Swan of Winter .	38
Aphorism: Mystery	38

CONTENTS.

	PAGE
A Wild Tiger-Lily	39
I Love My Love in the Morning	40
The Whoop-Crane's Clangor	41
The Mock-Bird	43
Women Poets	44
The Hospital at Night	45
Aphorism: Life	45
The Gods Are Dead	46
Cleopatra	47
Storm-Heart	49
By Mouths of Sea Worms Quaintly Carven	50
The Voice of the Turtle	51
A Little Rambling Rill	52
No Flag	55
Aphorism: Love of Others	56
Sonnet to a White Lady	57
Desert Voices	58
Autumn	59
Ingle-Low	59
Aphorism: Key of Pleasure	59
Wild Roses and Maiden Hair	60
Nature and I Are Glad	61
Reverie	62
Cherry Blossoms	63
Aphorism: Luck in Love	63
Hail, Comrade!	64
"Liberty Enlightening the World"	67
My Women	68
A Winter Morning Walk	69
A Fair Woman's Hair	70
Storm Lesson	71
Aphorism: Genius	72
My Witch Flames	73

CONTENTS.

	PAGE
IN A CEMETERY	74
APHORISM: PERFECTION IN NATURE	75
LOVE WAS RED	75
HOMELESS	77
IN A PRISM	77
EPICUREAN	81
SELF	82
I DRIFTED LIKE A WIND-BLOWN LEAF TO-DAY	82
A FACE SERENE	83
EVENING	84
A SONG OF SAD LOVE	85
BALLAD OF THE GREEN, GREEN SEA	92
THE LATTER DAYS	94
ONE HAPPY HOUR	94
CHOCOLATE	95
YOU STOOD	95
APHORISM: POETRY	96
A LARGER LIFE	96
GREATNESS	97
CRANFORD WATER	98
APHORISM: LOVE	98
PLACE ME AGAIN, I PRAY, GREAT FATE!	98
A SOUVENIR VILLANELLE	99
THE VALLEY OF SILENCE	100
THE LITTLE BROWN OWL	100
TRIOLET	101
OF AUTUMN WINE	102
THE DISINHERITED	103
LOVE IS A RIDDLE	104
AN IDYL OF THE BEACH	105
AN IDYL OF THE HILLS	105
SUNSET ON HOPATCONG	106
APHORISM: RECONCILIATION	106

CONTENTS.

	PAGE
FIREFLIES	107
THE LODGE	108
SCARLET TANAGER	108
I DREAM IN THE AMBER AUTUMN	109
ANEW	110
TO LIFT ONE'S HEAD	110
APHORISM: HEALTH	111
A TROPIC HOPE	112
A MEMORY SWEET	119
A KNIFE OF AGATE	120
SO WE CARE NOT	121
THE MELODY	122
THERE ARE LOVES AND LOVES	123
TWENTY KISSES	123
MY SOUTH	124
APHORISM: JOY OF THE MOMENT	125
BLACK ROBIN	125
A DREAM OF DREE	126
THE SYLVAN SINGERS	127
THE WORLD	130
SOUL AND SOIL	131
ONE MORE SONG	131

PROEM

Give me a finding thought, a subtle state, a vivid word!
Let me within the veil and let me learn!—
With every sun that burneth to its hills of sleep I burn,
With every leaping lightning flash I yearn;—
Let all this beauty be with me and grow
Until the open sesame of secret joy I know,
Until I tremble with the deep surprise, and stirred,
Can pipe full-throated music like a bird!

Ah, would that I might be a singer, too!
That this half-kindled music in my soul
Might burn melodiously athwart the scroll
Of human memories, in fadeless view!—
Touching to joy the lutes of life anew,
Re-echoed long where kindred spirits meet,
Where high endeavors mock at toil-worn feet,
And restless natures noble aims pursue!

I would my song could kiss with lover's lips!
Could weave all charms whereby mens thoughts are drawn,
And speak to shaken hearts a guiding word!—
My lay could paint the sea with wind-sped ships,
Paint waiting skies with herald fires of dawn,
And breathe a bugle note to souls unstirred!

THE WIND-HARP SONG.

I SING a wind-harp song,
  Dreamily musical,
Strange and faint and clear;
Beneath the steady stars,
Thro' the dim, sweet night,
Floating,
Mystically floating.

List!—
O listen!

The petaled stars are blooming,
In the skies, serenely lifting;
Their light in the weird woods faintly falling;
The dark woods, dim and damp,
Where the fern leaves droop,
And all the trees stand waiting,
Silent, alive, waiting
Till you have gone
And they may whisper and shiver
And move at will.

But now they watch,
With their many eyes, attentive,
Gravely silent and waiting,
Knowing much and remembering.

When you have gone,
Then will they beckon and whisper,
Stealthily, stealthily,
Murmuring sagas olden.

Old, old things they remember,
Of the burnt-out years,
Which, past-ward,
Like smoke-puffs, dim, are drifting;—
In fine ineffable whispers,
Each to each, they utter
Stories of battle and murder;
Beasts and birds and their hunting;
(The dead bones, buried beneath,
Their roots are sluggishly sucking);
Black nights and sobbing tempests;
The weeping of rain;
Long lights and shadows of mornings;
And sultry, slumberous noons.

In the still nights
The owl,
Soundless from tree to tree
Flitting,
Hears it all, and ponders,
Till his eyes grow great with wonder,
On his head the feathers rise,
Solemnly ponders,
Filled with wonder and wierdness and laughter.

The winds,
Whistling,
Singing,
From far away winging,

Tell their tales of Thence and Thither,
And Yonder Lands,
Over the Sun-fall Hills,
The Sun-rise Sea.

And the dusky winds,
Trailing thro' the black, vague
Negative
Of Night ;—
Winds woven from spirits, flitting ;
The breath of panthers ;
Of murdered men smitten down in the darkness ;
Of lovers sighing "closer !—closer !"
In warm bowers under the moon,
Secretly pressing flesh against flesh ;
Zephyrs from waving wings of vampires,
Kissing, pricking, drinking the warm blood ;
Air currents, rippling tremulous
From myriad motions
Of multitudinous creatures—
Running, leaping, crawling, flying,
Citizens of the void, mysterious,
Situate between the pulses of life called Day ;
Steams ;
Malaries from the marshes ;
Dreams ;—
Tell also all the wisdom,
All the romance of their substance.

And the stars
Fling down
Ineffable music,
Tinkling like jewels,
From all their aerial dancing.

And the moon
Burns a white and singing flame;
Singing of mystery,
Madness,
Love,
The burning of beautiful eyes
Uplifted,
And the slow, electric sliding of hands,
Tremulous,
Thrilling,
Caressive.

  * * * * * *

Notes of the wind-harp song
In the star-ray,
The fish-scale glitter,
The rainbow over the fountain,
The black shadow,
The moon's mystery,
The wind's whisper,
The brazen note of the great crane;
The fine voices
Of growing grasses,
Armorous flowers,
Motherly fruit,
Seed laughter;

Banks,
Bees,
Bird music,
Clouds,
Distance . . . .

Sleep.

THE WISH OF WOMANHOOD.

> THIS is the secret wish,
>   The prayer of womanhood:—
> "Give me a friend who reads my heart!
> Let me be understood!"

IN TOUCH.

TRUE natures are in touch
  With all things beautiful—
The earth and sea and sky,
Winds,
Wildlings,
And each other.

Their loneliness is such
As solitude relieves,
Art,
Or the rare, sweet reprieves
Of souls, akin,
Close met.

> Every woman is an undiscovered country.

MY DEAD.

AND you are dead, my beautiful, beloved,
  My inmost love, my sweet, dark, gentle friend;
No more the light from your brown eyes, so soft,
Shall be the radiance of my humble home;
No more your voice shall welcome back from toil;
No more your soft, brown, clinging tress shall frame
With glinting, silken charm your sweetest face;
No more that head upon my breast shall lie,
With fragrant breath perfuming all my beard—
Soul-beautiful, I would have died for thee!

No more!—I mind we often talked of death,
How that our final change was like a sleep
In which we dreamed ourselves away, away,
Into the stream that sparkled in the sun,
Into the breeze that whispered in the pine,
The bud, the blade, the inconstant flower,
The mobile cloud that dappled heaven's dome,
The lightning's flame that split the leafy oak,
The soft blue haze that hid in sylvan shades,
Away, away, till we were wholly gone;
Forming new life within a hundred lives;
Held fast within the circles infinite;
Unconscious, oft, that we had lived before;
Ofttimes unknowing we were living still;
Absorbed into the members of the Whole—
Nirvana.

   Ah! It was not wise to weep,
We said, in this short life so strangely sweet,

(I have not wept) or make a moan at death
(I have not moaned), but calmly, healthfully,
With conscious joy, we each should pluck the blooms
Within our reach ; and calmly, restfully,
Each one, when tired, should fall on sleep in peace,
Without regret or fear, as knowing well
The worth and worthlessness of life.

       O sweet,
O wise, without regret or fear you slept ;
And I—looked camly on your dying face,
And I looked calmly in your open grave ;
Calmly I go to reap the fruits of life,
Within the precious hours I keep awake,
This brief, swift-changing time that I am *man*,
Until I too shall sleep.

       O love, O sweet,—
Perchance within our dreams to meet !—mayhap
To kiss and flow together in the stream,
To laugh and murmur 'neath the mossy stone,
To drift and eddy in the placid pool,
Our eyes in bubbles smiling side by side ;
Mayhap to rise, sun-lifted, in the steam,
To float above the green, beneath the blue,
To fall in dancing drops upon the corn,
To flash in forking flames athwart the night,
Or call, or whisper, in the whirling wind ;

 It may be I shall swell the piping throat
That sings beside some sylvan nest, while you
May warm the breast that warms the spotted eggs ;
Just as I sang, erstwhile, in wildwood home,
When you, at eve, were with our nesting babes—
Ah well ! Farewell ! My lips repeat our lore :—

Be brave, be wise, be happy—this is *life*—
You taught in death, I live to teach it true;—
Soul-beautiful! beloved! I would have died
For thee! I would have *lived* for thee.

THE SOUL SUPREME.

I SING of a vision far,
   Of a thought on high things set,
   Of a sight serene,
   And a purpose clean,—
A pleasure in all things, great and small,
Loves and loss and the fates that fall,—
   Power to hold or forget.
  (*The fountains are clear as spar!*)

   Of the happy-wise, sing I.
     Consciously, ever to add;
     With their search sublime
     Thro' space and time,
Their solemn delight in all things true,
Their child-like joy in all things new,
     Simple and sweet and glad.
  (*Cloudless and blue the sky.*)

   The Overlook my theme,
     And the life in the Lifted Land;
     Where the nights have balm,
     And the days are calm,
The passions serve, and the charms obey,
And the brain is sane that holdeth sway,
     Gentle and firm the hand.
  (*Is it but a dream?*)

FREEDOM.

I sing of the soul supreme,
  Of a spirit erect and free,
    Too far above
    To be harmed by love,
Or fear, or hate, or gain, or loss,
Or to stake its joy on a gambler's toss,
  Hold self-empery.
  (*How the white peaks gleam.*)

CUPID.

O CUPID is a honey-bee,
    So it seems to me,
With a secret sting
And much honey :

In rosy hours,
Ravisher of flowers
In dainty bowers :

Musical of wing,
Builder of fair homes,
Yet roams
With dalliance, he.

FREEDOM.

FREEDOM is this to me—
    The Remedy.

I AM GLAD—ARE NOT YOU?

WHEN all is done, and there are none to love me,
When all is done, and flowers bloom above me,
When all is done, and all men shall forget me,
When all is done, and naught of fate can fret me—

All the East will flush as fairly as it now does, in
    the mornings;
All the birds will sing as sweetly, spite of Death
    and all his warnings;
Lips will kiss and hearts go thrilling, spite of
Time's ironic scornings,
    Then, as now!

    I am glad it will be so—
        Are not you?
    I am glad the streams will flow
        As they do;
    I am glad the sun will shine,
    And the vines will bloom and twine,
    And the autumn spill its wine
        Through and through,
        Just the same,
    Whether you and I exist,
    Or are not so much as mist,
    Or the memory of a name
        Men allow.

ONLY A MEMORY.

ONLY a memory is the maid
    Who loved me true in the young-love days,
The wandering days of light and shade,
Of toil and search in devious ways—
Ah!—little thought I she would be
    Only a memory.

Only a memory every charm,—
The music gone with the passing breath,
Each swaying grace of act and form
Forever still in the couch of Death;
Oh dearest love!—are you to me
    Only a memory?

Only a memory, tone and word,
The tender care of the thoughful brain,
The gentle touch that my spirit stirred,
The woman's ruth at the world's wide pain,
The dauntless will that *would* be free—
    Only a memory.

* * * * * * *

To labor and love is life sublime;
To labor and load an argosy
Sailing away on the tides of Time
To the shores of a dim Futurity,
To sail and serve when we shall be
    Only a memory.

Our ships float on, my parted love,
White their sails on a sun-kissed sea,—
The waves below and the winds above,
Waft our freights to the would-be-free,—
To sail and serve when sunk are we—
    Only a memory.

MY LADY GENTLE WONDERFUL.

GENTLE, wonderful is my fair,
  My sweet dark love with the unnamed charm,
With the clinging cloud of dusky hair,
Deep welling eyes of tender care,
    And magnet arm.

Gentle, wonderful is her touch,
  The silk-soft thrill of her little hand,
O who can tell why its spell is such !
Or tell at all why it means so much,
    Simple yet grand.

Gentle, wonderful is her voice—
  I have in my store no figure fit ;
I can but tell that it fixt my choice ;
I can but say that the winds rejoice
    To carry it.

THE GREEK ANTHOLOGY.

O BEATIFUL, bright Greeks, naked, flower-
crowned,
Elate with strength and grace of human life,
Types, evermore, of naturalness in man,
And rosy, fresh and dewy things in youth,—
To me thy gem-like songs are full of light.

The grace of bleating kids and fawns that skip
Upon the outlined rocks and peaks against
The opal sky of dawn is theirs ; the flush
Of sunrise pink upon the marble cliffs ;
The wash and drowsy lap, most musical,
Of waves rippling the blue, Aegean sea ;
The bubbling laugh of fountained nymphs among
Thy hills, rising to greet the morning sun ;
The song of blackbirds in the myrtle groves ;
The fluting of the little satyr lads
That herd thy goats and bask about thy rocks ;
The sanity of joy ; the dignity
And charm of simple, healthful life ; the mirth
And beauteous blossoming of freeest love ;
Wisdom most true, and penetrative wit.

TRUE LOVE.

What is true love? Is it this:
   Only on one mouth to kiss?

Only on one breast to lie?
Only for one touch to sigh?

Only in one soul to be
Shrined in love's idolatry?

To have and and hold a human heart
Sole for self, a slave, apart?

Is this true love? It may be;
It is not true love to me.

Love most true is this, I deem:
To, in love, be what I seem;

To be always true to trust,
Though the years go back to dust;

To be like a harboring bay,
Where my loves, at anchor, may

Lie forevermore, secure,
In a love that will endure;

To speak, in love, the simple truth
Tenderly, in manly ruth

Of a woman's agony,
Should Love speak deceivingly;

To be always frank and clear
To the hearts that hold me dear,

Though they love, and love again,
Others of the sons of men,

Though the lips that I may know
On still other lips may glow,

Though another love is first,
My love must not be the worst.

What my lovers love to me
Appeals for generous sympathy.

As they change not, nor will I,
But will give the sure reply.

Making answer aye the same,
When in love they speak my name,

When they call me, calling clear:
"Love, O hear me!" .... "I am here!"

   *   *   *   *   *   *

This is true love, large and free,
Love's *reliability*.

DEATH'S WORD.

FOR Death, but one word hath full eloquence,
   That great unvoiceable whose name saith—
      Silence.

   *   *   *   *   *   *   *

But one word holds all eloquence of Death:—
That undefined, unspeakable, which Silence saith.

MOTHER.

O MOTHER, calm and kind,
   The Friend of Peace,
Lo, you have found at last
   The long release.

Musing, we say farewell,
   For what is Death?
Or why does man receive
   Or lose his breath?

There is no answer here,
   Nor anywhere,
In earth, or sea, or sky,
   Or upper air.

We live in mystery,
   And when we die
No answer has the Sphinx
   To quest or cry.

We act our little part,
   Or well or ill,
Then pass with pallid lips
   Forever still.

We gag our clamorous doubts
   With platitudes,
And stoutly feign the faith
   That still eludes.

But whether we believe,
   Or feign we do,
We all remain the same—
   We do not know.

Faith is but willful hope,
   And proofless still ;
Faith never changed a fact
   And never will.

The simple ever hold
   That virtue saves ;
The good go down, they say,
   To blameless graves.

Ah, mother, you were wise
   When that you said
You troubled not tho' all
   The dead were dead.

For if the dead woke not
   Their sleep endured,
And life had sickness, oft,
   That nothing cured.

It did not trouble you,
   Nor does it me,
Whether we live so long,
   Or endlessly.

Life must be aye the same,
   Both gold and dross,
Virtue and vice, joy, pain,
   And gain with loss.

In earth, or heaven, or hell
  The law must hold,
The see-saw rise and fall
  With rhythm old.

And, mother, you have seen
  The all of it,
Ten billion years, I deem,
  Could add no whit.

But it may be you find
  Continued life,
Another world of joy
  And care and strife.

Or it may be you sleep
  The utter sleep;
Forever from the crowd
  Who laugh and weep.

*   *   *   *   *   *

Your life was very sad,
  But very sweet,
You walked in peaceful paths
  With gentle feet.

You made an atmosphere
  Of kindly grace,
You were beloved by all
  That saw your face.

You taught us to be true,
  As you were true,
To face the naked soul
  And look it through.

I thank you for that word,
　　Nor can forget,
Farewell!—most faithful friend—
　　My "mother" yet.

MAY, 1892.

EMILY DICKINSON.

IT seems to me you sing a song
　　That startled every one;
Odd intergrowth of heathen
And New England Puritan.

Your art is like a Japanesque;—
Perspective and detail
Are very independent,
But the picture pleases well.

Suppose a Quaker wood-bird
To throw a parrot wing,
Talk Manx and Hindostanee,
And then go back and sing

Wierd bits and beautiful,
A Concord touch or two,
Lyric thought, so stated
As no one else dare do.

REMEMBER.

DEAR friend, remember how we walked this Park,
All safe in very heart of fierce New York,
And felt the bright sun with the winds of Spring,
And saw, to-day, the late snow on the grass,
And saw, the next, the dandelions appear,
And marked the robin's breast against the green.

Remember how I read you verses in these nooks,
Hard by the little pool among the rocks,
Where ran the music of the little stream,
And your soft tones made music sweeter still :

Remember how we wooed the squirrels to come,
And saw the seals, and gave the "beasties" sweets,
And talked of gentle things, and things remote from man ;
And talked of simple things, and joys that have no sting ;
Letting our hearts flow on like little brooks
That sing beneath the sun, and were as gods
Or little children, free and wandering here,—
And knew the Gentle Life and felt the Great Content.

THE SMELL OF RAIN-WET EARTH.

THE smell of rain-wet earth upon the air,
   And rose leaves, wet and flashing :
The fragrance floats me back, all unaware,—
I see that love-white face divinely fair
Again—and drooping head with braided hair—
Half know the fountain plashing,
The smell of rain-wet earth upon the air,
And rose leaves wet and flashing.

THE MOON-SHARK.

IN the evening sky, to the eastward, thro' cloud
   waves long and dark,
The half-moon's tip was cutting like the fin of a
   golden shark.

MOUNT WALT WHITMAN.

WHAT! is Walt Whitman dead?
    Nay, it cannot be, for the mountains do not
       die!
They say he is dead, but the difference does not
       appear;
For he is a mountain,
A great gray rock,
Rugged, alone, forever;
And the mountains endure, sublime, motionless,
       and fixed before us;
They touch the sky, and we must see them, and we
       cannot forget.

Have you ever considered how marvelous a mountain is?
With its white head among the stars,
Its foundations broad as the bases of all things,
Deep as the center of the world's heart;
A witness of all, and of the order of all,
Surveying the centuries, and the scratches man
       makes in the surface of things, and the coming
       and going, like shadows, of the nations:
Familiar with the red whips of the lightning, and
       the deep-throated thunder;
With night, and the great tempests, and the wide
       winds of destiny;
The changing worlds of vapor, the awful solitudes
       under the stars, and the white, mysterious
       movings of moonlight:

Full of great voices, solemn music, sweet songs,
and the embracing silences of the upper air;
The roar of avalanches, the screams of eagles, the
melody of falling streams, the love-whistle of
little birds nesting by the blue tarns—
The blue tarns among the gray rocks (the wild fowl
know them) girt with green pines, placid, re-
flecting like mirrors :
Rich with mines of the white ore and the yellow,
Iron for strength, and coal for heat,
And radiant, glittering gems :

With slopes and valleys where vines grow, and
flocks feed, and hamlets nestle :

And over all, and with all, always the free air and
the wide view.

Ah, Walt, Walt, poet of Nature, comrade of free
men,
Other poets have been Olympian,
But you are Olympus itself.

MARCH 28, 1892.

ROBERT BLOOMFIELD.

INCARNATE voice of English May,
  The gentlest of the sons of song;—
As some soft brook to me, alway,
Thou art, O voice of English May.
'Mid rural scenes, in limpid play,
  I love with thee to float along—
Incarnate voice of English May,
  And gentlest of the sons of song.

AZTEC OF THE AIR.

AZTEC of the air, blithe Bob O'Link,—
  Quez-cat-a-lotl, link-a-link-a-link!
    Thy syllables, so sweet,
        I think,
Chime with the tongue of Popocatapetl,
And the clink-a-link-clink,
    Of a shaken sheet
Of crinkling, musical metal.

POETRY.

O POETRY,
　Thou art to me
My confidante,
My friend!

When all the tides within
Rise overflowing,
Thou art to me
Like liberty.

On thine infinity
My argosy
Is launched, a boat
With every tide.

But some will sink,
And some—who knows!—
O Poetry, thou art to me
As destiny!

THE DAY-BIRTH.

BEAUTIFUL!
                Beautiful!
                                Far away
The Sun leaps up with his baby, Day,—
A royal father, and proud, is he,
His visage gleams with fatherly glee;
The wood-birds sing and the roosters cheer;
The green leaves glitter—up starts the deer!
All nature rings with the glad refrain:
" Behold!—the world is new again."

THE WHITE SWAN OF WINTER.

THE white swan of winter is plucking her breast;
  With down-fluffs the hill rocks are padded and pressed;
    The cold winds are blowing,
    The white feathers strowing;
The white swan of winter is making her nest.

In all the universe but *one great fact* I see:—
Mystery.

A WILD TIGER-LILY.

A LURID Tiger-lily, flower of flame,
With purple blackness lurking in thy leopard
    spots,
And red-coal-ashed-with-gold-dust anther tips,—
Thou mindest me—I know not hardly why—
    Of one dear name,
    And one dark cheek,
Alike to thee in lovely arrogance of tint.
    Yet difference I spy
    In this, O fair flame-lily,
    All thy glories glint
    Within the lonely wood,
    Or hillside solitude,
Where some rare lover of the wilderness may roam
    Who only giveth thee caress,
    Who only thee may know;
    While *she* would glow
Where crowded-close humanity
Like over-ripe, packed peaches rots,
    And woman sips
The false, thin, flattering foam
From empty hearts upwhirled.

But still, when deeper cause for this I seek,
This line of likeness which I needs must guess,
I find in these things still you are the same:
An equal, rich luxuriance of life in both, I see,
And careless blazing of bold beauty on the world.

I LOVE MY LOVE IN THE MORNING.

SWEETHEART, lie still upon my breast,
With love-red lips to mine impressed,
And satin limbs that twine with mine,
Like clinging tendrils of a vine.

O, love, the morning 'gins to peep,
The rainbow-robèd cataracts leap,
A spotted fawn stands in the glade,
The dew-drop diamonds gem each blade.

Sweet love, I feel your gentle heart
Throb where the spherèd bosoms part;
My necklace rare, your warm white arms,
My coverlet, disheveled charms.

The whoop-crane's clangor wakes the fens,
Thrush voices pulse in echoing glens,
On wave-wet sands the sea birds meet,
Shy violets hide 'neath clover sweet.

Ah man is man, and maid is maid,
Sweet echoes, by each other swayed;—
Soft eyes will smile, red lips will cling,
Till Death his last scythe stroke shall swing.

The wild-fowl wedge through Northern skies,
In Indian glades the tiger sighs,
The siroc whirls the desert sands—
Love touches all, all climes, all lands.

THE WHOOP-CRANE'S CLANGOR.

ALONG the lone Floridian fens,
   Wild scrub-wreathed sands and hammock
      Edens,
Croaks the importunate, clanging cry,
From out the painted sunset sky,
Of whoop-cranes, as they roost-ward fly.

So when the level fire-lance ray,
The first swift glance of hot-browed Day,
Adown the moss-hung forest hall
Of bannered pines, plume-tipped and tall,
About whose roots the saw-palms sprawl,

Illumes the smoke-like vapor, blue,
Upsteaming all the lilies through,
And glancing o'er the waters, far,
Proclaims Apollo's coming car,
And warns all sleepers wake to war—

'Tis then that harsh and yearning sound,
Re-echoes to the morning's bound,
Clangs through the solemn cypress cave,
Warns the great owl his breath to save,
And shakes the bulrush o'er the wave;

As 'long the still and steaming pool,
Clouded with shadows, broad and cool,
These great birds fan impetuous wing;
While 'round them echoes fiercely ring,
And startled mock-birds cease to sing.

Prone 'mong the lilies 'long the shore,
The 'gator stops his blubbering roar,
And sets his still, reptilian eye
Upon these corsairs, as they fly,
Then heaves his vast, resounding sigh.

And yonder, where the hot rays fall,
A file of cooters, great and small,
Emboss the twisted pitch-knot log,
(Outjutting from the reedy bog),
Their black necks stretching, all agog.

Above, against a sapphire sky,
The osprey wheels his spirals, high;
His clear eye drinking all the sight,
His long wings glancing in the light,
His silvern belly flashing white.

Below, beneath the bay tree's shade,
The moccasin his length has laid
Of mottled char and muddy ash,
Still as the latent lightning flash—
They come!—and o'er him waters plash!

The small-fry note their coming, too,
And swiftly fin them out of view;
With startled croak the pied frogs leap,
The hidden lizard's bright eyes peep,
The newts among the mosses creep.

   * * * * *

The wide swamp lies at sultry noon
Beneath the brazen sun a-swoon;
All still, save yonder tall-necked crane,
Stalking with stately, watchful mien
Athwart the lily-burdened plain.

Pacing his stealthy, measured way,
In ashen plumage, dim and gray,
'Mid flowers, weeds and maid-cane grass;
Ghost-like he seems to fade and pass
From out the field of eye and glass.

  * * * * *

Thou art my pride, fierce royal bird,
No sound in Nature hath so stirred
The wild, free echoes in my breast,
As thy weird trumpeting's unrest,
A savage longing, sweet exprest.

THE MOCK-BIRD.

ABOVE the white magnolia bloom
 The mock-bird trills and sings
A woven note of lightsome 'lume,
That lights the cypress-cavern's gloom
 And through the palm top rings.

The morning sun is in his eye,
 His breast stands to the light;
All morrow cares he doth defy,
Hope helps him perch above them high,
 Beyond them take his flight.

Now, suddenly, I see him rise,
 Cresting a wave of song;
Then swiftly falling, far he flies,
With white-barred wings and love-bright eyes,
 The hammock's edge along.

A gift hath to his lady borne
   In their bright sylvan room,
A nest, 'mid orange leaf and thorn
(All open to the Orient morn)
   And citrus bridal bloom.

I hear their twitterings sweet and low
   Behind the emerald screen;
I hear a flower of music grow
That dims those bells and buds of snow
   With all their scent and sheen.

Sweet solace of the Southern home,
   The bird I love the best;
Within thy brain some mirthful gnome
Sure bids thee brew this mocking foam
   Poured sparkling from thy breast.

WOMEN POETS.

O WOMAN! Poem alive, to me;
   I wonder not you are unversed in *verserie*—
Can a poem itself make poetry?

THE HOSPITAL AT NIGHT.

Roosevelt, Midnight, April 8th, 1889.

I SIT within the long dim ward at night;
   Around me silent beds or snores or groans,—
  Ah! List that prayer with anguish in its tones:
"O God, God, God! How soon will it be light!"
"Kape sthill! An' let us shlape. Oi think yees
    moight!"—
A boy asleep, who smiles, (with broken bones)
Dreaming of mother or some playground sight.
  Without, thick darkness and a wind that moans.

A rattling breath, a gasp, a still, white stare,
   A nurse's jest: "Discharged—tie up the jaw,
    A label on the wrist to save mistakes,"
The tramp of dead-house men of heedless air,
   Two lines of lifted faces full of awe—
    A sickened sot, that cot to-morrow shakes.

Life is an agreement of contradictions.

THE GODS ARE DEAD.

THE gods are dead, and only shrines remain;
The gods are dead, but still the Christs are slain;
The gods are dead, but priests yet work their will;
The gods are dead, but men must worship still.

The gods are dead, but Mystery is yet,
And fears and tears and drops of bitter sweat,
And these begot and these have slain the gods,
And these upheld and these shall break the rods.

The gods we made to help us in our need,
And gave them crowns and in their lips a creed,
But Pain crushed on and they helped not at all,
And so we turned and smiled to see them fall.

We in our minds make all things that we know
Of gods above or god-like powers below:
Kings, tyrants, lawyers, warrior or priest,
The millions serving and the few at feast.

Withhold our faith and all these things shall fall;
Like as the gods to whom our faith was all;
Make change within and outward there shall be
Fair field, free growth, and life in all things free.

CLEOPATRA.

RECLINING in her chamber sat
    Egypt's great queen,
Below, on skin-of-tiger mat,
    There might be seen
A fair slave, prone, to stool her feet.

Her carven couch was rich with gold,
    And flashing gems
Were bound upon her forehead bold
    And on the hems
Of all her royal robes replete.

The walls were wonderful about
    With pictured things:
Isis, Osiris, battle rout
    And pride of Kings—
Ptolomy, Menes, Pharoah.

Out thro' the open window, far,
    Her fierce eyes swept
The fertile land, thoughtful of war;
    While shimmering slept
The corn beneath the noon-tide glow.

The hand that pressed her satin flank
    Was clenching tight,
And thro' pale lips that twitched and shrank,
    A gleam of white
Showed tigress teeth set hard at Fate.

"What!—shall I be a thing of scorn
    At Cæsar's show,
I, at whose feet, with sighs forlorn,
    Not long ago,
Rome's proudest knelt to supplicate?

"By Isis!—no!—if steel can stab
    Or poison slay,
No tattling mob my shame shall blab
    Thro' Rome that day!
For I have reigned . . . and now . . . can die.

"What say'st thou there!—a peasant brings
    A crate of fruit?
'Tis well—bring here. (Now lord of kings
    Thy mob may hoot,
With this friend's help I thee defy.)

"My ladies, leave me . . . thou too . . . all,
    For I would sleep.
(Sooth a heavy sleep methinks 'twill fall—
    Ah, I could weep!
But royal pride hath heart of stone.)

"Quick now! . . . kind goddess, give me strength!
    Up with the lid!—
Uprears that green and glittering length,
    Out it has slid—
O curse my fear! . . here! . . strike! . . *'tis done.*

"Bless thee, dear snake! Ah, I love thee!
    That little bite
Makes free. Now Rome, what shall me dree?
    In thy despite
I 'scape; thou canst not me demean.

"A deadly langour clogs each vein,
   My limbs grow numb;
Now shall I sleep . . . Anthony! . . . no pain . . .
   Ho! Roman scum!
Laugh at yourselves . . I die . . a . . queen."

STORM-HEART.

TO live in the quick life of the wind!—ah!
   Knowest thou not the joy of the breath of life
In the nostrils of the swift man, air cleaving;
In the deep lungs of the galloping horse,
Rushing impetuously onward, neighing,
Spurning the resounding earth with beating hoofs?

Canst thou not exult, with me, with the mad waves,
Leaping, flashing, foaming, upflinging spray;
With the boom of the surf upon the shore;
The wrack of clouds in the sky, storm-beaten;
The flapping of the sea-bird in the gale;
And the long wail of the winter wind
Thro' the wild throats of the darkened pines?

To live in the wind, to move, to sway with it,
Rising and falling with its noble rhythms,
Surges and lulls of the great gales—Ah me!
Ever since I was a boy I have felt thus.
I have loved the storm, and the speed of winds,
The run of waves, and the black heart of tempests.

O wings of the great winds, whirling, whistling,
O serpents of flame,
   O voices of terror,
      O breaths of tempest,
         Storm-hearts, I love you!—
As the dark eagles of the mountains,
As the fierce, wild falcons of the desert,
As the sea-gulls flashing over the breakers,
As the stormy petrels of the black seas.

    *   *   *   *   *   *

To be God-shot by the long lightnings,
In the great forest, by the still, stern rocks,
With the thunder muttering and exulting,
With the wind sobbing and the rain weeping,
The pall of a black cloud overhanging,
And the torn leaves drifting over, alone—
Would not that be a beautiful death to die!

BY MOUTHS OF SEA WORMS QUAINTLY CARVEN.

A LITTLE sea shell
   From the beach,
By mouths of sea worms quaintly carven,
  Whispered me a thing to tell:
    "Loving is living!"
  Whispered well,
  Whispered me, and slipt and fell
    Into water, out of reach.

THE VOICE OF THE TURTLE.

I AM a dove,
    The bird of Love,
And the woodlands ring
When I sing ;
  I do not mourn,
    I rejoice,
  When the little ones are born
    I lift my voice :

Coo-oo! coo-oo! coo-oo!
For the mate I love and woo,
For the nestlings, two,
    Coo-oo!

    And I croon
    At sultry noon,
In the coolness and the shade
Of the glade—
  O do not say I mourn,
    Or am sad,
  I have life and love and corn,
    I am glad.

Coo-oo! coo-oo! coo-oo!
Dear mate, fond and true,
I have life and I have you—
    Coo-oo!

A LITTLE RAMBLING RILL.

O MAIDEN fair
   In hair
And face and form—
Ah, how the blushing warm
   Blood
   Makes flushing flood
Thro' all the sweet lip-pasture of her cheek !—
   O hear me speak !

   Hear me declare
   Confession, bare,
   Of all my fondness true
   For you,
   My azure sky's white dove,
   My love,
   My goddess bright
   As light.

   Hear me proclaim,
   Aflame,
   My ardency
   For thee.
   That little fleck
Of curling hair, behind, upon your neck,
   Entangleth me—
   Make me not free !

   O maiden sweet,
   Discreet,

A LITTLE RAMBLING RILL.

Why should so long the blisses
Of warm kisses
Abide,
And hide,
Where your two lips, sweet,
Meet?

O maiden pure,
Demure,
Why should your soft bright eye's
Surprise
Be veilèd back—
Alack!—
By kissing of fringèd lids, dainty, down
Thrown?

O maiden coy!—
Ah, joy!—
Now little smiles,
At whiles,
Begin to creep,
Peep,
And show thro' rippling lips your teeth
Beneath.

Ah, now your tender eyes
In love arise;
And softly speak
That what I seek
You gladly give.—
O darling! now I live.—
My sweet one, come
Home!

Your timid, tender kiss
Is bliss ;
Like new rain on the earth
In time of dearth ;
Your clinging half-embrace
Makes race
Thro' every vein
Sweet sense of gain.

Upon my cheek your breath
In silence saith
A sweeter thing
Than sirens sing,
When like winds whirling,
Wandering,
They flee
With moonlit feet along the sea.

Your little hand's
Soft nestling stands
My heart still with full pleasure ;
No measure
Have I for my joy,
Without alloy.
I cannot speak for peace,
So cease.

NO FLAG.

NAY, I am no patriot ; not for me
This prejudice, so proud, of one's own country,
Always right, chiefest cause of enmity

Atween the nations. Were it not for this,
All peoples had a million years, I wis,
Ago, exchanged of brotherhood the kiss !

And, were it not for this, how great a flood
Had never flowed of warmest, reddest blood,
From hearts of murdered heroes, brave and good !

How many women hearts unbroke had been,
Had " patriots " not forgotten they were men,
And murdered that their land might "glory" win !

O folly, this, to die to wear a tag !
O crime, to kill because one's country's flag
Is different from some other piebald rag !

For noble hearts find one land scant of room,
All men their brothers, and the world their home,
From highest mountain peak to ocean foam.

Their love holds all, their boast is every clime,
Their sympathy with every race in every time,
All patriot songs with equal voice they chime.

They lift no flag, and sound no party cry,
And leave to fools to run in herds to die,
Insane at hearing : "Foreign foes are nigh !"

For them there are no foreigners at all,
No prejudice of birth, no Chinese wall,
The Briton but the fellow of the Gaul.

They hold all roads are open, earth and sea,
No rightful duty, tax, or passport fee,
All travelers welcome, and all commerce free.

They would all bounds were blotted, bars were down
All nation-lines and States were overthrown,
Naught left but honest neighborhoods alone ;

For honest men no laws, no government,
No interference, howsoe'er well-meant,
Each man's life, fortune, as he pleases spent.

O when shall men be tall enough to see
That pride of country makes for slavery,
That he alone who has no flag is free !

The man without a country 'habits all ;
Without a flag all banners drape his wall ;
His patriot heart hears but the wide world's call.

Love others *because* you love yourself.

SONNET TO A WHITE LADY.

O SAD White Lady of my soul, I say,
   Listening at memory as one might the spell
  Breathing mysterious from some twinèd shell,
Wherefore art thou so far from me astray?—
So far, and yet so close to me alway
   That my own heart seems but thy house, to dwell
  Awaiting thee, and all my soul thy well
For thee to drink—so strange!—ah, well-a-day!

I mind me now of some whose souls have bent
Like bows, full aimed upon some great event;
And so have broken, missing what they meant;
Disarmed, and yet with arrows all unspent.—
And some who, meeting Love without dissent
For once, have kissed and kissing died in full content.

DESERT VOICES.

O DESERT voices, why tempt my soul?
  For what have I of kin with thee?—
With deadly sun and the drifting sand,
  The cactus-thorn and the blasted tree?

Ye desert voices, why tempt ye me?
  For aye and ever I hear ye call:
"O come, where the wastes are wild and wide,
  And the wide, wild winds are over all!"

O desert voices! O Great Sublime!—
  My soul is moved by thy weird appeal;
Force unknowable, unmasked Life,
  And the Seeds of All Things in thee I feel.

    *   *   *   *   *   *

The heated sand and the pallid snow,
  The sullen mountains, bare and tall,
The fierce and beautiful, bitter sea,
  And the wild, wide winds that are breath of all.

AUTUMN.

THE season, like a courtesan,
    Hides her age with paint and gems,
Dyes her locks with gold.
Pleasing hard while please she can :—
Lovers hasten !—no delay !
She is smiling, warm as May,
Quickly passeth charm and sway,
Glare and glory fade to gray,
Naught at last but leafless stems,
And the end is cold.

INGLE-LOW.

BLESS you fire, born of burned wood !—
    For you bless me and do me good ;—
Antic and lightsome and kindly and warm,
You make in merry when out is storm ;
And no man finds him a blither friend
Than his ingle-low, at the hard day's end.

The key of pleasure —appreciation.

WILD ROSES AND MAIDEN HAIR.

THAT she was warm I was aware,
With all sweet virtues in her air,
(*Wild roses and maiden hair.*)

Night has morning and night has noon;
Woman's face is a hidden rune
(*In a hammock, beneath the moon.*)

So it were hidden she did not care;
Her dress was white, in the moonlight, there.
(*Wild roses and maiden hair.*)

Her feet were dainty in slippered shoon,
The trellis-vine had a fragrant swoon.
(*In a hammock, beneath the moon.*)

The little hands were soft and bare,
I might have touched them, but did not dare.
(*Wild roses and maiden hair.*)

The end was coming and came too soon!—
Words unspoken, and never a boon!
(*In a hammock, beneath the moon.*)

NATURE AND I ARE GLAD.

THE days are leaden and purple in stain,
    And laced with bars of a sweet, dark rain,
And the brows of men are heavy with pain,
    But Nature and I are glad.

The fields are sketched and etched in gray,
With charcoal shadows of night-in-day—
O why do men hate such?—tell me, pray!
    For Nature and I are glad.

These warm, wet days are akin with the South,
And they kiss close down, like a wet, warm mouth.
You may pray, if you will, for the days of drouth,
    But Nature and I are glad.

They are filled, a-thrill with the thunder-soul,
The pen of the lightning has writ their scroll,
And brows may furrow, and lips condole,
    But Nature and I are glad.

For the days are latticed with sweet, dark rain,
They are gray and purple and leaden in stain;
Dull hearts get dolor, dull lungs complain,
    But Nature and I are glad.

REVERIE.

I SAT me down within a beauteous wood,
All in a strangely sweet and dreamy mood,
My thoughts, like all those bright leaves, strewed.

I drank the freshness of the amber air,
The glowing beauty of those colors rare,
And thought of one whose face was dark, yet fair.

'Twas then a nymph-like form beside me stood—
Is it a sylvan spirit of the wood?
Or is the wine of autumn in my blood?

The ripeness of the time my soul receives,
An Oriental web the sunshine weaves,
Rich-hued, and patterned by the crimson leaves.

A gentle presence shares my pleasure now,
The glory of the day gleams on another's brow,
Our thoughts are far too deep for words' light flow.

Ask not, O friends, that I should tell you more;
There are sweet secrets in the heart's deep core,
Close guarded as the mine's rich ore.

CHERRY BLOSSOMS.

CHERRY blossoms are white and sweet,
    As a white cloud from the sky come down,
White as fair foam from the sea upthrown,
    For the eye's joy meet.

Cherry blossoms are white and sweet,
A dark-red the robin's breast among,
And full of red love the song he sung—
    My love sings discreet!

Cherry blossoms are white and sweet;
The far, fair sky shines blue between,
And the sharp, bright air seems washed out clean—
    Summer whispereth!

Cherry blossoms are white and sweet,
Thunder and sun and ropes of rain,
Anger and smiles and kisses of pain,
    Petals blown with a breath.

There is luck in love where the woman woos.

HAIL, COMRADE!

WRITTEN FOR EVALD HAMMAR'S FORTIETH BIRTHDAY, OCT. 3RD, 1892.

HAIL, comrade, whom my thought endears,
Your day of birth, of forty years,
Deserves a bit of rhyme!

For we were chums, in heart and thought,
Among that little band who sought
The Southern clime

To hold a larger life and free,
In the elect society
Of thinkers great.

Who came to browse on Eden food
And lead a life of brotherhood—
Millenial state.

Alas, we only found it true
That names oft change, but seldom do
The hearts of men;

The bigot is the bigot, still,
Whatever words his mouth may fill,
Of generous ken;

The pard doth not evict his spot,
Nor blanch his hide the Hottentot,
Because his name

Is changed from this to something else,
Or some brave tag the public tells
   His whitened fame.

And thus we found the fact to be,
A "Liberal" might be aught but free,
   And for "Reform,"

It might be but another creed,
To limit nature, cripple deed,
   And mind deform.

*   *   *   *   *

You built your home, and I built mine,
From logs of hewn and peelèd pine
   And cleared the land

Of saw-palm, pine, and black-jack oak
And planted what we might to cloak
   The naked sand.

Remember you those long-drawn days
Of flashing sun and azure haze
   And balmy air,

When we would toil with plow and hoe
To coax the lazy trees to grow,
   The crops to bear?

And those gay nights when all would meet
To kick out care with dancing feet
   And rustic mirth?

Or when, within my home, you'd sing
And make the little fiddle ring
   Beside the hearth?

Those days were hard ones for us all,
And yet I love them to recall,
   For there was much

That gave us pleasure in them, too,
And every thought and purpose true
   Found us in touch.

Our thoughts were high, our speech was great,
With noble hopes we were elate,
   And every plan

To make life freer, wiser, strong,
Was in our ears as some sweet song
   Of help to man.

You were a teacher to me, there;
You opened doors to fresher air
   And gave me food

To ease my hunger for the best,
And that of which I was in quest
   You showed was good.

Among that small, Utopian band
You were my chiefest, chosen friend,
   And when you left

It seemed our music left with you;
My fiddle strings all snapt in two,
   Of you bereft.

   *   *   *   *   *

Well, friend, those times are past and gone,
And you the fortieth mile-stone
   Are reaching, fast,

Upon life's journey to that strange,
Unravelled mystery of change
   Of all the last.

I wish you birthdays, many more!
Of all good things I wish you store!—
   And, ere you die,

May your glad eyes perceive, fulfilled,
The freedom they have wished and willed—
   And so—good-bye!

"LIBERTY ENLIGHTENING THE WORLD."

HARD by the ferry's rail I stood, one night,
   And saw the beacon gleam across the bay,
Of that fair statue bravely raised to say:—
O Brain and Hand be Free!—in words of light;
But as I looked, no statue met my sight,
Only a shapeless shade that seemed to stay
Atween the glorious torch-star, sweet as day,
And where the pedestal shone palely white.

A symbol this, it seemed to me; forsooth
The world lies wan beneath high Freedom's flame,
And, dazzled, knows not yet her form, nor grace;
Her torch to men is but a torch in truth,
Few read as yet her lines of healing fame—
Too dark! Too soon!—the morrow sees her face.

MY WOMEN.

BEHOLD *my* women, grave and sweet,
With eyes of depth, and stately feet.

With brows of thought, and magnet hand,
And tact and heart to understand;

Who hear and see, and quickly feel,
What tone and glance alone reveal.

Who, hand in hand, keep step and stride,
With tender courage, at my side.

Who fit my mood, as fits the sea
Into a noontide reverie.

Who calm my soul, as does the sky
When on the sward I musing lie.

Who give me rest, as Mother Earth
When on her breast I make my berth.

Whose woman's pride and kindling eye
Inspire me like a prophecy.

Whose courage high, and faith elate,
Bend all my aims to nobler fate.

Who stir and thrill like music, rare,
And cleanse and free like ocean air.

Who bid me trust them, have no fear,
With lips of truth and eyes sincere.

I know my women, grave and sweet,
And they know me, where'er we meet.

A WINTER MORNING WALK.

THE gray hills circle on the bourne of sight,
    And like a picture on a shell are drawn
The eastward farm and trees upon the light:
    Across the pallid, drifting fields of snow
    I stride, elate, while overhead the crow,
    Cut on their clearness like a cameo,
Athwart the pearl-hued skies of first, faint dawn,
Flaps like a flying fragment of the Night.

Hold we but hope of souls untouched of tether,
    And pace in step with Nature's mood alway,
        For health and wit and happy thought and love,
No matter be it fair or falling weather,
    Or skies be black or skies be bright above,
    The morning is our youth, and spring of day.

A FAIR WOMAN'S HAIR.

BEWARE
Of the spell of a fair woman's hair!
Glinting with sun-gold.
Floating in air,
Softer than silk of the Orient loom,
Brown, auburn, or golden, or glossy in gloom;
Fragrant, beautiful snare;
Beware
Of the charm of a fair woman's hair.

Beware!
The bonds of the heart are there;
Curling so prettily over the brow—
Oh turn your eyes from its magic now!
Those threads are the strings of Cupid's bow,
His arrows dart from bright orbs below:
Turn!
Spurn!
Or your heart will yearn,
And your thoughts will burn—
Ah! when will the wise man learn
To beware
Of the snare
Of a fair woman's hair?

Beware!
Take care!
A lasso of Love is each hair,
Waving and crinkling there,

Or bright and straight
With the beauty of Fate;
Brittle as glass yet strong as steel,
Entangling hearts for woe or weal;
Drawing a man to the gates of sin
Or hedging him in
With a holy veil,
Against which Hell's gates cannot prevail—
O hide me there!
Safe from care,
Wrapt in the cloud of a fair woman's hair,
Beautiful, beautiful hair.

STORM-LESSON.

I.

AGAINST the sombre pines the white storm whirls,
  Below a felted sky, wan-hued as death,
  While all the woods are rimed with Winter's breath,
The trunks ice-mailed; sleet cuts; the wild wind hurls
  The damp and clogging flakes, and rhythmic sings,
In wailing words of chanted under-song,
  As in the lee the wave-like drift it flings,
A rune of things unfathomed, old and strange and strong.

II.

The East is pale as pearl ; faint stripes of red,
   Athwart, burn clear and fine, the fields are white
   And drawn with drifts curl-lipped like shells ; the Night
Hath banished Storm ; the Winds, wide-winged, are fled,
   And with the sun, lo !—all the world hath gems
And fire of stabbing sparks and jewels a-cling
   To crystal twigs and spangled sprays and stems—
While tinkling on the crust the falling ice-casts ring.

III.

O Nature, mother, sweet and fierce and kind,
   Strange, beautiful or passionate or grave,
   From thee are all the things that slay or save,
That give us ease or dread, that loose or bind ;
   And, we, of thee begotten, have the germs
And rudiments of that thy largeness hath.
   Thou canst no more, and I accept thy terms
And wage with thee no silly war of whining wrath.

Genius is intuition, innate force and the passionate desire to do a perfect thing.

MY WITCH FLAMES.

THE witch, Flame, stept on a kindling stick,
    And leapt with a bound to the apex, quick,
Scattering abroad her blazing hair,
Waving weird arms, wild, red, and bare.

Tossing her smoke-blue mantle o'er,
With a crackling laugh, half-hiss, half-roar,
Licking the logs with her lapping tongue,
Writhing, worm-like, the knots among.

While eerie urchins came from her wame,
Skipping some step of an elfin game,
Doing the tricks of their demon dam,
As apes, insane, with an oriflamb.

And their red eyes winked, 'mid ashes gray,
As they turned and squirmed and vanished away
Stretching, anon, like tip-tailed snake,
Lizard-like, seeming to fall and break.

So I sit and pore at the eldritch race
And their flapping fun in that sooty place,
And hold my toes to the genial heat,
Or nod and grin at a witch-face, sweet.

But it sometimes seems that they stay not there,
But leap and climb in my beard and hair,
Bedaubing my nose with charcoal grimes,
Whirling my wits in mad-cap rhymes.

* * * * * *

Ay, I love ye well, ye witch-flames, gay,
As I sit at mine ingle and mind your play—
May ye and I be friends for long
Ye skip-jig Muses of my song.

IN A CEMETERY.*

I SAT among the earthed and speechless dead,
   While in the west the great sun, round and red,
Sank like a sign behind the hazy hills.

My thoughts were floated far in solemn trance,
The heights of life and death stood in my glance
   And all the vale that intervening fills.

The giggling laugh smote faint upon my ear
Of thoughtless ones who jested there, anear,
   While on the bourne the day's life burned out clear.

A dry wind, lingering, touched upon my brow,
And seemed to whisper: "Work your worth out now,
   For all the hope of man you see below.

"'Tween hills of dawn and dark a little vale,
A little day before the light shall fail,
   And then oblivion, soundless, swift and pale."

O mystery of joy and all held dear!
O mystery of pain and death and fear!
   O mystery of all we may not know!

---
*Hillside Cemetery, Plainfield, New Jersey.

And yet I scarcely long to have it less,
I love the music of its awfulness,
 The solemn cadence of its rhythmic flow.

> It is right (saith Nature) to seek perfection, but wrong to attain it.

LOVE WAS RED.

O LOVE was red, and Love was ripe,
 And Love shone like the sun,
And my brain went round with a sweet delight,
As I sped away through the charmèd night
 With the maid, my lovèd one.

Her eyes shone bright till the stars went pale,
 Her hair was silk-of-gold,
Her cheeks were hot with the blushing blood,
Her lips were full, like the red rose-bud,
 Her voice was rich and bold.

"Come! love of mine," she sweetly said,
 "And bear me far away
Upon your steed so strong and fleet,
Away thro' the moonlight, weird and sweet,
 Long miles ere break of day!

"For my home is not a home to me,
 My parents are cold and stern;
My soul revolts at this tyranny!
O take me hence, for I would be free!
 With love for you I burn!"

My mare stood under the linden tree—
　　Black as a flashing coal—
And she pawed the ground as she saw us come,
Whinneying low a glad welcòme,
　　As tho' the maid were her foal.

I placed my love on a pillion soft,
　　With one white arm she clung—
Her warm breath played athwart my cheek
And words of love in my ear did speak—
　　Ah me!—our hearts were young.

Afar we fled through that moony night,
　　And landscapes strange and still;
And the hills rose up and the hills sank down,
As we galloped on past waste and town,
　　Till midnight clocks did peal.

We reined, at last, in a forest lone—
　　My cloak was wide and warm;
Where love is pure and love is real,
Where hearts are warm and hearts are leal,
　　What matters a bond, or form?

Our priest was Love who gave the ring—
　　The circle of joy complete—
By Nature's rites our souls were wed;
And the stars looked down on our sylvan bed
　　And danced with twinkling feet.

Yea, holier far than prayer of priest
　　Is the maiden's kiss of love;
And the faith of a true and sincere man
Was never yet helped by Statute's plan
　　Where Liberty smiled above.

HOMELESS.

WHOSO hath home hath hope,
    A wall of courage at his back,
A coigne of vantage for his feet,
And for his head a rest.

Whoso hath home hath hope:
The beasts upon the thousand hills
Have all and one a cuddling place,
A hole or nest for each.

———

Whoso home hath none is sadder than a beast,
As poor as Christ, and lonelier than a fox.

IN A PRISM.

I WOULD write me a poem to-night,
  Gemmed with beautiful words;
    But of what,
    I know not;
I have only the impulse aright,
    The passion to sing,
Like the waves and the birds;
    And the thought
    Is not clear,
Nor the vision to the seer,

But I write
As one might
In prophecy
Unsought,
And I think, it may be,
As bards of minstrelsy
Improvise.

Arise,
O my soul,
Come out!
There is music in thy brain
Like the rain;
Like the laugh
And the sip
Of the lip
Of the wave
On the sand.
It is faint, like the mist,
And it turns
Like the wind that we list,
And it burns
Like the flush of the flame in the womb
Of the time when the daytime is not.

I sat on the ground
To-day,
With a hound;
And he was the brother of me.
Exceedingly
Beautiful were his eyes;
Gentle and merry and brown.
Ah it was sweet to be down
On a level with him and all things there
In the grass.

IN A PRISM.

We, who are tall,
How much of pleasure we pass!
Of the joy which the little and earth-close know!
Is it not so?

There is place for me,
Discovery,
Wonder, adventure and mystery,
In the forests of ragweed and clover,
In the *silvas* of the grass;
Where the beetles roam,
And the butterfly hovereth over,
The humming-bird is ruby lightning and thunder,
The toad is a gnome,
The pebble a rock,
The harlequin-spider swings his silvery net,
Dew-wet
On the fret,
And to us, thereunder,
The tall lily is goodlier than the palm.

O soul,
There is room!
We are free!
In the inness of things there is room,
There is room in the wind and the sea,
There is room in the crowds of the tree,
In the multitudes of the grass.
There is welcome for me
In the beauty of things;
In the sunset
I am home.

Did you ever swim in the sky?
Often have I,

And hung in the air like a kite,
I could turn to the left or the right,
And go
Or high or low
In the atmosphere
Of crystal.
Come up with me there!
We will fly
To the top of the purple cloud
Where the shrill hawk circles;
We will sit on the golden verge;
We will feel the urge
Of the winds of the world;
We will see the crimson stain the side
Of the cliffs we ride;
We will have sight,
Aright,
Like the high gods,
Tall,
Over all.

O soul,
I surmise
We are too achromatic.
Would it not be wise,
Sometimes,
To live in radiant rainbows?
In the Iris-land perfume is food,
Music is breath,
Color is sight,
The winds are what eloquence saith;
Love is the moon of the night,
Glamour her light;
For stars, beautiful eyes,

And for sunrise
A smile.
O would
It not, for a while,
Be well
To dwell
In a prism?

EPICUREAN.

AH!—sing glad heart, sing
Thy pean;—
There is but one wisdom, even joy
And kindly wishing!
Well saith the Epicurean:—
To-day be happy, for to-morrow die
Thou must.
Therefore to-day is glad perfectness of life,
Breath,
Innocence, and happy-hearted laughter,
With manly earnestness of strife;
To-morrow cometh sweet Death,
The blending with the dear brown dust,
And—how think you?—nothing after?

SELF.

To be sufficient unto self!—to me,
   Who fain would stand on purest heights serene,
Where suns rise first, sink last, and all is clean,
This seems the acme of philosophy,
The one great need of whoso would be free:
   Mine own sure friend, no matter how demean
   My fellow selves, nor what may come between,
I know no lack of love, nor sympathy.
With reverence still before myself to stand,
   To learn, to love, to honor all therein,
   Knowing self-injury alone as sin,
And sin to others, sin at second-hand—
I deem a sane man's thought, and therefore grand,
   The attitude of one whom truth helps win.

I DRIFTED LIKE A WIND-BLOWN LEAF TO-DAY.

I DRIFTED like a wind-blown leaf to-day,
   Along a rambling, country, back-roadway,
Whose unkempt banks and bed as red as rust,
And white stones scattered in its ruddy dust,
Were toned with autumn sunlight's mellow ray,
That soft, on all things like a glamour lay,
And russet hue of leaves, which every gust
Of wind sent whirling with imperious *must*.

A giant mastiff, gentle, by my side,
With lion-front and hue of eye and hide,
Was comrade with me, happy, wandering there,
Blown onward by the wanton piercing air,
Marking with me, approved, the gray and green
Of cedars and of farmsteads quaint that flanked
the scene.

A FACE SERENE.

I WOULD my face were as a god's in mien,
  Not proud, nor pitiless, nor taint with scorn,
But calm, illuminate with joy inborn;
The face of one whose eyes to smile are seen
As deep, still fountains, crystal-clear and clean,
  Hold visions sweet of blue-sky peace 'mid thorn
  And crag of rudest wilderness, uptorn;
"Self peace!—To others peace!" from depths
serene.
Ah! beautiful are lips that restful move,
  And strong, smooth brows that fairly, calmly
think,
  And gentle eyes whose courage is to death;
The fair, strong features whoso sees must love,
  The firm, strong hands that with yours truly link,
    The pleasant mouth whence cometh Truth's
sweet breath.

EVENING.

A PLAQUE of gold, up slips the moon
  Above the shadeful eastern hills;
Far-floating, like a big balloon,
  Its pale light crimping on the rills.

The little stars come twitching out,
  Like spiders on a sky-blue wall,
Twinkling their little legs about—
  See there!—that one just had a fall.

Each firefly strikes his little light
  And joins him to the gay quadrille;
Brisk, eager bats flap through the night;
  We all receipt mosquitoes' bill.

The whip-poor-will's clear sounding note
  Comes echoing from the black-caved wood
Where great, wise owls silent float,
  Or screech and hoot in comic mood.

*   *   *   *   *   *

The oars dip softly in the mere,
  A girl's light laugh thrills on the breeze,
Rich, murmuring tones come to the ear—
  What import have such sounds as these?

The wavelets ripple by the prow,
  The moonbeams sparkle on her hair,
His form is bending toward her now,
  And—we had better leave them there.

A SONG OF SAD LOVE.

O DEAREST love of mine!
   Thou lovest not to kill,
But it must be
That cruelty
Is deep in thee.
For oft thy moods incline
My heart to spill,
My hopes to tease.

Though all thy charms so please,
I can not hope for ease
With thee, but pain,
For it is plain
Thy sweet eyes find delight
In my sad plight
And baffled suit.

The fruit
Of Tantalus
Thy grace
For all my prayer;
With half-averted face,
And smiling eye,
Thou, careless,
Hearest my sigh,
And hold,
O beautiful! but cold,
My love in light esteem—
Ah, foolishly I dream!—
Thou wilt not spare.

O pity me,
For it must be
That I should so love thee!
Man cannot 'scape his fate,
Nor soon, nor late,
Be other than he must.

* * * *

And yet I trust
And dare to hope;
Before me there doth ope,
Like as the mirage, fair, might cheat the sight
Of one upon the desert sand,
Such vistas of delight,
With groves of peace,
And springs of calm content,
As make me raptured stand,
And give me no surcease
Of longings, theeward spent.

I weary thee
With all these plaintive moans,
And this my love-sick air;
And yet so dreamily
Thou listenest my tones,
And eke my tender prayer,
That I may not forbear,—

I am not wont to supplicate,
But such is now my fate!

Ah, Soul within my soul!
O Heart-beat of my heart!
If we must live apart
There is no perfect anywhere,
And all my days shall wear

A SONG OF SAD LOVE.

This sorrow like a thorn,
And all fields shall me warn:
"Yea, this too must be borne"—
What shall me then console!

Presumptious is my love,
Thou art so much above,
So better, everyway, than I,
And yet I cannot still this cry,
My great need makes me bold,
I may not rest my heart
Till all of it is told.

My love hath this one art
Of poetry;
I needs must sing to thee:
Most like the love-smit bird,
Whose ardent notes are heard,
From shaken throat, elate,
Imploring, wooingly,
His coy, reluctant mate.

O love, we are so near
In every hope and fear,
In every dream and thought,
And all that thou dost state
Hath kindredship so clear
To somewhat I have wrought,
That I am moved to build,
Audaciously,
Whilst thou art kind to me,
Before thy sight
The visions that I see
With pleasuance filled
Of our delight.

* * * *

I meet thee, O my fair,
In vernal woods,
Among the birds,
And note the soft surprise
Leap to thy cheek,
The lovely lips that speak,
And eloquent, sad eyes.
We go a-rambling there,
The trees among
And emerald fields,
Where blades and buds are young,
The day is young,
The year,
The flowers that have upsprung,
And we in heart, my dear.

Like children, so we stand,
Hand clasped in hand,
Beside the forest pool,
Or gather mosses, cool,
Among the ferns ;
Or take the devious turns
Which ever hath
A woodland path.
While woodsy fragrance yields
From leaves, damp mold, or brake,
At every step we take.

I gather flowers there
To twine within thy hair,
And bring thee guerdon, strange,
Of lichen, toadstool,
Frond,

A SONG OF SAD LOVE.

The bleachèd tortoise-shell,
The club-moss from the pond,
The Indian-pipe's pale bell,
And such like simple spoil
Of woodland range
And sylvan soil.

For thou art good to me,
Thy tones are sweet,
(On this our holiday
And treat),
Thy features, erst so sad,
Wear now no care,
For Nature's sympathy
And, it mayhap, my own,
Hath ta'en all away,
And left thee glad
With joy in life alone.

I lead thee to a seat
On fallen log
And cast me at thy feet—
The blackbirds whistle sweet
Around the bog—
And, when I lift mine eyes
I see thy dear face there,
Bent down as from the skies—
My angel!—true and fair.

* * * *

'Tis slumberous afternoon
In June,
And I, in easy chair,
Read thee a pleasant tale ;
Swinging thy hammock, where,

Beneath the shadeful trees,
All murmurous with bees,
The languid calm of summer thro' us thrills.

The banks within the vale
Quiver with heat;
The distant hills,
From our breeze-drawn retreat,
Before thy dreamy gaze,
Melt in an azure haze.

A-swing
With gentlest motioning,
At ease,
Thou, upward, through the trees,
Perceivest swallows twittering fly
With fluttering wing,
And graceful dip and spring,
Against the dark-blue sky;
While Alp-clouds pile them high
Within the widening West.

Lo, all is Sabbath rest!
And yet
Holds threat
Of thunder by and by,
When Night,
With Shadow, draweth nigh
To fright
The Light
And put out sight.

*　　*　　*　　*

I sit beside thee, dear,
And hold thy hand;

We speak not any word,
For all the night is grand
With flames we do not fear,
And over all is heard
The thunder's breaking roar,
And rushing, swift downpour
Upon the roofs of rain.

We feel the solemn charm
Of midnight and of storm—
An organ strain—
And are as one in twain,
For thou art close to me,
Reclining on my breast,
And in my sphere of calm
Is all thy soul at rest.

A gently stroking hand
Hath loosed fatigue's close band,
And drowsy fancies creep
Upon the sense,
Like as a little child,
Within some sure defence
Of sheltering arms,
Secure from all alarms,
To Dreamland is beguiled,
Thou art a-nest.

The thunder's muttering threat
Dies far away;
Upon the mountains wet
Its echoes play;
I lie awake and hear
The gentle rain
Soft beating on the roof
And window pane;

I may not sleep at all
For deep content,
For ended is my call,
Thou art no more aloof,
My loss hath turned to gain,
And all my breast
Is with fair locks besprent,
Where thy dear head is pressed,
In breathings soft and deep,
Of utter sleep.

BALLAD OF THE GREEN, GREEN SEA.

I MET a milk-white woman there,
   Down in the depths of the green, green sea,
Wrapped in a net of her red-gold hair—
   She threw its mantle over me.

Her breasts like great foam-bubbles were,
   Down in the depths of the green, green sea,
And pearls were strung on her red-gold hair,
   In the woven net that compassed me.

"O whence come you that seek me here,
   Down in the depths of the green, green sea?"
"I am a dead man, drowned anear;
   O who are you that speaks to me?"

Her eyes were blue as the deep water,
   With a phosphor gleam thro' the green sea,—
A wonderful, beautiful sea-daughter,
   Swaying and smiling there at me.

BALLAD OF THE GREEN SEA.

"O I was drowned an hundred years
    Ago, in the depths of the green sea,
And all these pearls are all my tears,
    And in this net I drowndèd me.

"An hundred years ago we sailed,
    Out over the depths of this green sea;
A corsair crew—O fate bewailed!—
    Struck us and slew all souls but me.

"And me they stript to taste my shame,
    And wove a net of my hair on me,
I 'scaped, and leapt like a blushing flame
    Into the depths of the green, green sea.

"Now you have come to be my love,
    Down in the depths of this green, green sea,
To sleep in a cave in a coral grove—
    O come, dear love, and lie with me!"

She wrapped me then in her mesh of hair,
    Down in the depths of the green, green sea;
A woman's tress is stronger than prayer,
    And never a prayer escapèd me.

Now happy the lives of us so dead,
    Down in the depths of the green, green sea;
Where still, slow currents smooth our bed,
    And I hold her, and she holds me.

THE LATTER DAYS.

OH cold and blithe are the latter days,
    When the winds go wandering round and round,
With the brown leaves drifting, nowhere bound,
And the skies are pale, and the hills a-haze,
And the rabbit leapeth before the hound.

The woods meseemeth a shipping's spars,
From the dead-leaf sea which the world hath drowned,—
If I were dead would my soul be found,
Playmate of winds and the dancing stars,
Tumbling the dead leaves over the ground?

ONE HAPPY HOUR.

ONE happy hour, one afternoon,
    I lay in my boat on the open bay,
Cradled and rocked by the rythmic sway
Of lapping and laughing waves at play,
Dreaming and dreaming whatever I would.

With pulses tripping a pleasant tune,
As young as ever, and life as fair,
A boy, on my back, with never a care,
Drinking the joy of the salt-sweet air—
"Live in the present, for Life is good!"

CHOCOLATE.

SWEET like a child, but wise, so wise ;
  A little brown woman with bright brown
    eyes ;
Piquant and charming ; magical bands
Weaving with eloquent, soft little hands,

Daintily, tenderly ; merry and sweet ;
Smiling and smiling from eyelash to feet ;—
Closer and closer, ever, to thee,—
O little brown woman, why winnest thou me ?

YOU STOOD.

YOU stood a sweet, still statue, looking down
  To see him pass ; the while your woman's
    heart
With him went too, and all your vibrant soul
Swung struggling with strange moods, and yet no
    word
Nor sign—" Good-bye ! "—O irony of Fate !

So might some lute, most daintily attuned
To lays of love, in soundless grief perceive
The only hand which knew the touch to strike
Its waiting music out to life, withdrawn :—

Come back! O touch me once again! Come back!

* * * * * *

O wonderful and sweet; why should you love him so!

Poetry is the rhythmical interpretation and expression of charm.

A LARGER LIFE.

WAKE to the dawn of a Larger Life,
   Sleepers dull in the Night of Now;
Beat your hearts to a wider strife,
   Build your thought in a broader brow!

For the hills are high that hold the sky,
   And the waters are wide that wash the world,
And the breaths of all men, that live or die,
   The winds have given and caught and whirled.

Be free and conscious of all you are,
   Dignity and a selfness great,
Life at one with the farthest star,
   With all of Nature in every state!

For the hills are high that hold the sky,
   And the waters are wide that wash the world,
And the breaths of all men, you and I,
   Forever and ever the winds have hurled.

GREATNESS.

SHALL a man always long for greatness and yet never attain it?
Shall he spend the treasure years of his life in training for great battles,
And then see his heart eaten with rust,
His hands soften with sloth?
Shall he lie like a log on the beach,
Stranded out of the currents of the great sea, forever?

Nay, it matters not!—
For this is greatness to be always ready for it.
It is not the great deed that makes the great man,
The deed is but the outward sign,
Not greatness but the publication of it;
For though the man be stripped, dumb, paralyzed,
He can still be great.
Greatness inheres in the great thought, the clear purpose, the serene poise, the wide view, the overlook;
In individuality, ability, reserve force, knack, courage, knowledge;
Not in what you have done, but in what you can and will do if need come.
The cannon may not speak for a decade,
But, if it be loaded,
It is always sublime, deadly, terrible.

* * * * * *

When the time comes—!

CRANFORD WATER.

AN ink-black flow beneath November's gray
   And serious sky:—upon it, as I stay
My listless footstep on a bridge, I spy
A dead leaf, sapless, drifting slowly by—
Still stream, brown leaf, bare branches pointing
   high!
And musing much I wend my aimless way.

All loves inspire—weak loves vanity and a willingness to deceive; great loves nobility and a passion to deserve.

PLACE ME AGAIN, I PRAY, GREAT FATE!

PLACE me again, I pray, great Fate,
   Beside a nature broad and grave and sweet!
To all my nobler thirsts and passions mate;
Inspired and sane again, great Fate,
Within the realm of some soul-queen, so great
   That Love himself, page-like, waits at her feet,
O place me once again, great Fate,
   Beside a nature broad and grave and sweet!

A SOUVENIR VILLANELLE.

IN an open boat on a winding stream,
   Lilies and flags and a flashing sun—
Do not forget how the waters gleam!

Souvenirs fit for a poet's theme,
   Gather we here where the ripples run
In an open boat on a winding stream.

Flowers and friends that we hold in esteem,
   Shall we remember when all is done?
Do not forget how the waters gleam!

Life is for all but a floating dream
   (Tallied by trophies, memory won,)
In an open boat on a winding stream.

Threat of storm and a bright sunbeam
   (How ends the voyage when once begun?)—
Do not forget how the waters gleam!

Are real things fairest, or things that seem?
   Shall we look back upon this one?—
In an open boat on a winding stream?—
Do not forget how the waters gleam!

THE VALLEY OF SILENCE.

BEYOND lies a valley of silence,
  Clear night without tempest or star,
Naught holding but darkness and stillness,
  And calmness that nothing can mar.

We go to that valley of silence,
  Days happy or sad bear us on,
Repose in that valley of silence,
  When joyance and sadness are done.

Peace, peaceful that valley of silence,
  Full of great words ever unsaid;
Pure silence, clear calmness, real resting—
  Sweet echoless vale of the dead.

THE LITTLE BROWN OWL.

THE little brown owl
  That sat in the tree—
With great, gold eyes
  He looked at me.

He laughed "Ho-Ho!" And I laughed "He-He!"
At that little brown owl that sat in the tree.

  The little brown owl,
    That sat in the tree,
  With gold-black eyes
    Winked thrice at me.

He laughed "Ho-Ho!" and I laughed "He-He!"
For I thought him a droll bird, certainlie.

>That little brown owl,
> That sat in the tree,
>Seemed over-wise
> Exceedinglie.

But he laughed "Ho-Ho!" and I laughed "He-He!"
At the solemn face he made in the tree.

>O little brown owl,
> Tell me, prithee,
>Why art thou so
> Solemcholie?

But he laughed "Ho-Ho!" till I laughed "He-He!"
And he spake me no more for a veritie.

TRIOLET.

To lie on one's back and look at the sky,
Up through the branches and leaves of green—
Why, I used to do that when only *so* high!
Lie on my back and look up at the sky,
At the white and the blue, and wish I could fly.
  It gives one a feeling so great and serene,
To lie on one's back and gaze at the sky,
  Up through the branches and leaves of green.

OF AUTUMN WINE.

Of autumn wine, sweet friends, I fain would sing;
That golden nectar, ether strained, doth sting
  My nerves, intoxicate, to brighter bliss
    Of brighter dreams than Madjoon slaves e'er wis
When from their pipes the white, slow smoke doth ring.

That topaz-hearted, amber drink forth bring
In crystal, variant-dyed by leaves a-swing,
  While dreamily we drain the bowls we kiss
    Of autumn wine.

About our halls an azure haze doth cling,
And on our walls are vagrant birds, whistling
  In music clear, their farewell songs—'tis this
  That bids me mind that somewhat we must miss
For every draught we quaff, with heedless fling,
    Of autumn wine.

THE DISINHERITED.

THEY cluster at every corner;
    They wearily pace the land;
Their starving eyes devour each loaf;
    They stretch the begging hand.

They are hungry and sick and tired;
    Their bleeding footsteps lag;
My brothers!—and none to help them!
    Their nakedness mocked with a rag!

They bake, and others have eaten;
    They burn, but others are warm;
They build, but their heads, unsheltered,
    Are bare to the pitiless storm.

They till, but the crop goes from them;
    They reap, but "The Harvest Home"
Means to them that their product is stolen;
    They brew, and taste but the foam.

Ah God!—how sadly they call Thee;
    If Thou wert, Thou couldst not withstand;
But always the wicked have triumphed;
    The cunning and strong rule the land.

The hearts of the mothers are breaking;
    The daughters are bedded with shame;
The fathers are brutish with labor;
    The thoughts of the sons are a flame.

And Hatred and Arson and Murder,
  Like demons they beckon and tempt,
The hand to the sword is outreaching—
  Blood! Blood!—O can nothing exempt!

O Wisdom be instant and help us!—
  Quick rearing thy radiant crest—
O brothers, *the sword is a traitor!*
  The calm, thoughtful methods are best.

The way of the wise is the best,
  Which thinkers have pondered and planned;
The Gordian tangles are slipping—
  Behold!—your release is at hand.

LOVE IS A RIDDLE.

LOVE came to me with a new-appearing head:
  "I see you do not know me," Love said,
"But I have many forms, and in no one am I
    altogether wed."
"You are truly very strange, Love," said I,
"You are never twice alike, and I cannot tell the
    why.
Tell me, sweet Love, are you always thus unlike
    and appareled differently?"
"Always," said Love, "lest men weary of me,
Lest with limits of 'I know,' they should hold me
    less than free."

AN IDYL OF THE BEACH.

BLUE sky, and in the distance sails, no cloud;
   A sea-bird winnowing the salty air;
A sweep of shining sand, a pebbly glare
Beneath the sun; foamed sea-dogs running loud
Upon the beach, choked sullen back, half-cowed;
   Knee-deep, two blue-clad women, walking there,
   And hand-in-hand, with shining, unbound hair,
Their faces strong and sweet, their motions proud.

A shell, upwashed, doth whisper in my ear:—
   "The sea—the sea hath washed full many hearts
     Their red love out, and left them cold and still."

But sun and sparkling wind wot not of fear,
   Nor those fair figures happily free of arts,
     To-day is joy—let morrows work their will!

AN IDYL OF THE HILLS.

I MIND me how I walked, one summer's day,
   Adown a hillside, straw-hat on my hair,
   Coat off and "pants" in boots, all debonair;
Bearing two pails for someone going my way,
Sunbonneted, in country girl's array,
   Demure, with plump hands berry-stained and bare
   And pleased shy eyes beneath a forehead fair,
While something glad about us seemed to play.

Well-met, and not quite all an accident,
   Though we were willing each should think as
      much,
      She capped the knoll as I the gap unrailed,
And subtle glamours all about us blent ;
   That braid of tawny hair I longed to touch,
      Yet loved the sweet half-fear that just pre-
         vailed.

SUNSET ON HOPATCONG.

PLACID, softly shaded as a dove's breast,
   A-tint with olive green where in it sink
Dark shadows of the hills along its brink,
As some gay bird is taken by its nest
The wide lake fills with all the painted West ;
   All mingled stains and tender lights a-link,
   Pale gold and flame of rose and flush of pink,
Gleam there ere droop the purple plumes to rest.

Entranced, I see some red Nariticong
   Dip paddle in those pools of sunset stain,
      His wild dark eye, beneath his eagle plumes,
Smiling a little at the chanted song
   His young squaw sings of happy hunting plain—
      A savage dream, which all the West illumes.

The more we grow the more we become at peace with the Universe, the more tolerantly we regard the motives and motions of others, the more restfully and contentedly we yield ourselves, to ourselves, the less we fear from *laissez faire*.

FIREFLIES.

I SAT at ease upon my latticed porch,
   While in the cloud-walled west the thunders smote
Their muffled drums and up the east 'gan float,
In globe of gold, sweet Luna's lover's torch,
While bats and bugs that dread the midday's scorch,
   Flew, chirped and hummed; and yonder in the womb
Of very night the fireflies lit the gloom
With sparks that mocked the lightning's sudden search.

You bring unto my memory thrillingly,
   Beloved insects, fitfully luminous,
      Visions of sultry evenings long ago,
         When by your light I marked her cheeks deep glow,
   As in the night my passion amorous
I breathed, and knew she listened willingly.

THE LODGE.

BEHOLD it!—thus:—a rude room ribbed with
    logs,
A puncheon floor, a roof of riven boards;
A fire-cave mouth of rocks, whose flame affords
The only, flickering light; two guant, sad dogs
Outstretched before, their dream of trails, banks,
    bogs,
Deer, fox, tongue-lapping streams, most fit ac-
    cords
With all that garniture of hunter's hoards—
Horns, flasks, pelts, guns, dirks, tools and trapper's
    togs.

The wood-wolf's bark wails wide beneath the
    moon,
That coldly paints a path upon the lake
To where the wild ducks sleep; the screech-owl
    trills,
All stealthily disports the barred raccoon,
The bucks come down and splash beside the brake
For on his robe snores now the *One-who-Kills*.

SCARLET TANAGER.

A SCARLET bird in a grass green lane,
    Glowing beneath the lilac-bloom;
In a crystal pool of the recent rain,
Flinging pearls from a preening plume.

I DREAM IN THE AMBER AUTUMN.

O I DREAM in the amber autumn,
    When the forests are filled with flame,
And the haze hangs blue on the mountains,
    And the days march ever the same.

When the palette is painted with sadness,
    Fire, sweetness and passionate breath,
On a background of purple distance,
    With the blood-tints and ashes of death.

When the wigwams of maize are awaiting
    For the spoiler to ravish their store,
And the brown leaves are rustling and drifting—
    A Dead Sea with never a shore.

I am tranced in the mellow misting
    Of the amorous atmosphere,
And the slumberous warmth and languor
    Of the smoky and golden air.

I am proud of the sumach and maple,
    Whose banners are crimson and gold
Tho' the days of their winter are coming
    And the days of their summer are told.

And I dream in at-one-ness with Nature,
    Stained through with her beauty and pain;
I am drunk with the wine of her color,
    With the pangs of her deaths I am slain.

ANEW.

A LISTENING stillness in the morning air,
   An air of night-shade, touched with coming fire,
With cooling freshness weaning my desire,
While new hopes paint their dawn on night's despair:
I kiss the sad sweet lips that are so fair,
   I read the tear-bright eyes that bravely smile,
   And her dear, quivering mouth that would beguile,
And count that woman-courage more than prayer.

O love, within this morning cool and new,
A new day riseth fair within my view!
   For you, to-day, I tread the purple crest
     Far, far above the passion-tainted plain;
   For you, henceforth, I do my manhood's best,
     And peace, like this bright dew, shall ease our pain.

TO LIFT ONE'S HEAD.

TO lift one's head on high, on high,
   And look beyond it all, afar,
The petty strife and party cry,
   The shallow spites, that jar, and jar;

TO LIFT ONE'S HEAD.

The narrow thoughts of partizans,
   So pitiable and yet so proud,
Self-deemed of truth the sole defence,
   The ear so shut, the mouth so loud.

The stupid bounds of sect and clan
   That think their little worlds hold all;
'Twould burst them to be large as man,
   And if they fail the heavens fall;

The childish formulas of creed,
   Babe-guesses petrified in faith—
"Oh weary, weary, weary breed!—
   O give me room!"—the free soul saith.

I lift my head on high, on high,
   And look beyond it all, afar,
To where the mountains touch the sky,
   And where the oceans beat the bar.

In health the essential word is *balance*, the method, *motion;* exercise, thorough, searching, all-inclusive; for the body running is the perfect exercise, for the mind, writing. A good runner—a vigorous, buoyant man; a good writer—a facile, well-educated man. In a nutshell—*Verbum sat sapienti.*

A TROPIC HOPE.

I HOLD, heart friends, a dream of years;
A visioned hope, dim seen through fears.

And this is how it dreams to me,
This flower-enwreathèd vagary: —

A summer isle in tropic clime,
With peaks volcanic, sharp, sublime,

That stab from out the level sea
And pierce the blue immensity

Of perfect azure, arching clear,
A wind-washed, sun-thrilled atmosphere;

While at their feet a cirque of white
And dazzling beach flames on the sight;

Whence, landward, calls a thunderous moan,
The sullen surf's deep monotone,

As curving, tumbling breakers roar,
And, foamy-lipped, suck at the shore.

And there, far up a mountain side,
'Mid jungles, cliffs and vistas wide,

(With bridle-path, a steepy stair,
Rock-edging, twisting, half in air,

A TROPIC HOPE.

Upwinding from the vale below)
A terrace hangs, whereto I go.

For on that shelf is built my cot
Of palm and cane, with roof inwrought

Of thatchèd leaves; with vines, intwined,
Which thatch and rafters joining bind;

With wattled walls that frame and hold,
And floor of smooth, down-beaten mold;

With unglazed windows, opening wide
Their shutters, that within may glide

The fresh, bloom-scented wind-of-trade,
To give cool hearts to noons of shade,

When, in verandahs low and deep,
My hammocks swing to dreamless sleep.

My furniture my own hands make
From knotted spoil of jungle brake,

Jointed bamboo and lustrous woods
Known but in tropic latitudes.

My floor with Indian mats is spread,
With netted guards swings free my bed.

And, all about, barbaric spoil,
Of seaside sport and jungle toil,

Adorn floor, ceiling, or the side,
Or on my shelves arranged abide:

Sea-beans and sponges, sea-shells rare,
Shark-jaws and beauteous corals fair;

A scarf of bark as fine as lace,
A mottled tortoise carapace;

The mailèd coat of cayman grim,
Flamingo-wing, and snake-fang slim;

Great beetles, transfixed with a pin,
A *coteau* sheathed in serpent skin;

Machetas, keen, with heavy blade;
Riatas, tough, of raw-hide braid;

A rifle cased in porpoise hide,
Fish rods, nets, harpoons, side by side;

Spy-glasses, pistols, fossils, gum
And reptiles bottled up in rum.

With goodly pictures here and there,
And books and papers everywhere.

My house-cat is a petted snake,
For fly-traps, lizard tongues I take.

Above, a screaming parrot swings,
Chased by a monkey through its rings.

Withon my board cool sherbets plash
In cups of gourd and calabash,

'Mong Creole baskets heaped with fruit,
Cassava leaves or arrow root,

A TROPIC HOPE.

Palm cabbage, sooth and delicate,
Rich sweet potatoes, yams of weight;

The milk of goat or cocoa-nut,
And honey combs of amber glut;

Delicious eggs my fowls have laid,
And fish by baited hook betrayed.

Without, my faithful dogs unite
To guard my dwelling day and night.

I have a cow, a pony, goats,
And on the beach behold my boats!

Ah! such as this is wealth indeed;
Fat grows Content where lean grows Need.

Happy the eye that clearly sees
The worth of wise simplicities;

Their wholesome comfort, *sans* pretence,
Their pleasing of the artist sense.

Eschew the love of luxury,
The simple life makes whole and free.

Beware the palace's thorned ease
Welcome the cabin's homely peace.

II.

Around my home there stands a grove
Of tropic palms and plants I love.

The orange and the sprawling fig,
The manihot, with tubers big;

Sweet grapes and olives rich with oil,
Guava's fruit that asks no toil;

The palm of dates, and cocoa-nut,
The banyan, whose strange limbs down-put

An hundred trunks, instead of one,
To bear its leaves against the sun;

Acacia-foliaged tamarind,
The lilac-flowered Pride of Ind;

Banana, very tree of life,
Plumed pampas-grass, each blade a knife;

The great silk-cotton's bole, butressed,
The royal palm of heavenward crest;

The passion flower and fruit divine,
The fragrant, fair vanilla vine;

The coy and shrinking mimosa
The flesh preserving *poypoya*;

The woman-breast-like pomegranite,
Coffee, matè and chocolate;

The cherimoya, luscious, sweet,
Whoso which tastes must surely eat;

Pine-apples, sweet as lady lips
When Creole kisses Cupid sips

In tropic-passioned ecstacy,
In tropic bowers, by Carib sea ;

Sweet lemons, limes and *sapota*,
Custard-apple and magnolia.

But ah ! my poem must not clog
Its music with this catalogue.

I will be brief and say but this
Of these my Eden bowers of bliss :

An hundred fruits and sweets are here,
Where want comes not, nor famine near ;

A thousand flowers bloom and scent
The zephyrs 'neath my fruit-grove's tent

Of wondrous foliage overthrown,
With ropes of sunlight lacing down.

III.

About my grove sharp hedges fret
Of needled Spanish bayonet ;

Or fence of giant cacti, high
A score of feet, tall cerei

With candelabrum arms beset,
Aflame with flowers when night-dews sweat.

Or thousand-handed prickly pear,
With cups of gold and weapons bare ;

Or massive agaves ranked in rows
Of mighty spears, defying foes.

And here are arbors deftly made
Of living bamboos, lattice-laid,

Their feathery foliage green between,
Bignonios netting close the screen.

And here are hammocks, gently swayed
Beneath the mango's perfect shade;

And here are paths of semi-gloom
'Neath arching oleander's bloom;

And here are vistas fair and far—
Inland, to mountain walls that bar,

Upward, to peaks in clearest air,
Downward—ah, dizzy ones, beware!

Seaward, o'er sweeps of boundless blue
To where the sky line stops the view;

The mountain walls and valley beds
The tumbling torrent's silvern threads;

The waves, the beach, the sails that pass—
All subject to my eye and glass.

Ah, faith!—it is a fair, fair dream,
And foolish, too, my good friends deem;

But then we live our lives but once
Each hath his bubble, sage or dunce,

And this is mine—then let me be !
Give me my isle, my tropic sea,

My hut upon a mountain steep,
My fruit groves where the trade winds sweep,

These simple joys, wealth without pelf,
My thoughts, my dreams, myself, *myself*.

A MEMORY SWEET.

I HAVE a memory, sweet and clear,
   Of a woman whose name was Rest ;
Who folded me in with warm, strong arms
Away from care and the world's alarms,
   Close down on her tranquil breast.

I have a memory, clear and sweet,
   With never a thought that mars,
Of tender lines 'round a sensitive mouth,
Dark eyes that tell of the tropic South,
   And midnight hair with sheen of stars.

I have a memory, still more sweet,
   Of her face aglow with joy,
Of joy because she stands near me—
Mon doux repose ! Ma chere chèrie !
   In our love there was no alloy.

I have a memory, passing sweet,
   Of a dance that was Motion's rest ;

Of our floating, 'neath the lovelight's gleam,
On the eddy and swirl of music's stream
   Together, breast to breast.

   O memory sweet,
   O vision dear,
   O spirit, kind,
   From Love's bright sphere—
   Why am I by thy presence blest?—
   My sweet Repose, my Love, my Rest.

A KNIFE OF AGATE.

LO!—a paper knife you send me of the agate of Ute Pass,
Smoky clouds and mossy branches in a crystal clear as glass,
In my pocket bid me place it, use it for my daily need,
'Tis a curio rare and dainty—thanks for it, dear friend, indeed!
But 'tis broken!—Well, I'll mend it—that shall be to us a sign
In our friendship: Yours the giving, but the mending must be mine
Should it break—to heal so deftly that a scar shall scarce appear
'Thwart the verdure of its mosses, on its field of agate clear.

SO WE CARE NOT.

AH, sweet Life, you cheat us always when we
put our trust in thee;
Only when we doubt and care not do you give us
gear and fee;
Only when we flout and scorn you do you treat us
tenderly;
Only when we build above you are we really rich
and free.

Like a woman, if you follow, she will turn and
walk away;
If you plead her heart is hardened and she only
answers "Nay;"
If you laugh and look beyond her she will closely
by you stay;
Let her find your heart is higher, she will court you
every day.

Seek for friends, and they forsake you; live for
love, you lose it all;
Live to love, and love will give you drink of ashes
steeped in gall;
Build your own, and all will aid you, so you build
not weak nor small,
Love your own and all will bring you loving gifts
to heap your hall.

THE MELODY.

O SING me the melody, sweet and low,
Of hearts that throb, of cheeks that glow,
Of the world transformed by a light divine
That out of beautiful eyes can shine.

Let a note there be of this mystery,—
How the hair on a girl's head witcheth me,
How the touch of a soft hand sets a-thrill
All the brain and nerves and the firm-set will.

Let one rhyme sing of the sweet surprise
When the lone heart mirrors in loving eyes,
When out of the cold and dark there form
Dear lips that kiss, dear hands so warm.

Let a word be heard of the tenderness
That a maid can show in a man's distress;
How all things else may a man forget—
Not a lovelit eye with its lashes wet.

O sing to me of this melody,
Music and rhythm and harmony,
Of hearts a-chime to the dancing joy
That rings from the string of the archer boy.

THERE ARE LOVES AND LOVES.

THERE are loves and loves that pass one by
　　As light as birds in a summer sky,
As sweet as flowers that quickly fade,
As little dreams, made and unmade.

Their memories linger—ah, how sweet!
But we hear no more their tripping feet;
The world laughs on, and we laugh too,
But we sigh sometimes, as all must do.

But loves there are, when we lay supine,
Which suddenly lift, as with touch divine;
And our lives grow rich with wealth untold,
And our nerves as bowstrings, twanging bold.

And these loves last, for their lines are deep;
Their days are sun-full, their nights are sleep;
With life they live, and they shape the breath
That lingers last on the lips at death.

TWENTY KISSES.

TWENTY kisses on your cheek,
　　Lady love, so fair;
Blush and pallor, hide-and-seek,
　　Prove them welcome there.

Twenty kisses on your throat,
    Dainty, round and white;
Swelling soft as love-tides float
    Innocent delight.

Twenty kisses on your lips—
    Little sweetheart, mine!—
As the bee its flower sips
    Thrills my mouth on thine.

Twenty kisses on your hair—
    Little darling, sweet!—
Could my love print plainer there,
    I would kiss your feet!

MY SOUTH.

RONDEL.

MY sweet warm South, strange woman of the sun;
  With breath of soft, sad winds blown from her mouth,
Dreamy with sighs; lovelier there is none—
  My sweet, warm South!

With bare, brown feet, bathed by perpetual youth,
She leadeth me through all her bowers to run—
  By solemn swamps, still streams, and dunes of drouth.

Lo!—I am Northern, yet, wonderful one!—
  I love her; crown her, seeing she allow'th,
With jasmine gold her hair of night outspun—
  My sweet, warm South!

This moment hath its own joy.

BLACK ROBIN.

A WORD for you too,
    Robin,
Black pony,
Beautiful,
Hard fighter;
Many the sharp tussle we have had together,
Many the flying gallop through the woods,
Along the shore road,
With glimpses through the trees of brown beach,
    white sails, and wide stretches of water.

"Now boy!—Come sir!"
"I will not!"—Kicks, plunges, short-stops, shies,
    head-down, back-running, curb-jerks, white-
    foam, sweat, keen cuts of the rawhide and
    sharp words of command;—
Brave boy!
Always beaten but never conquered:
Yet, after all, I fancy you did not hate the man who
    would not be thrown or troubled;

There was fighting friendship between us;
When I patted your proud neck you would look as
    if you liked me;
And you never took advantage of me when I threw
    the reins on your neck and trusted you;
And I never struck you without warning;
The gage of battle was always fairly given.

" Here, take this apple ! "—
Farewell Robin !
Stubborn, broad-browed, stout-hearted, fearful of
    nothing;
Cunning rogue,
Glossy fellow;
We shall go no more together.

A DREAM OF DREE.

I WENT and spoke to the wrinkled tree—
    Tell me, friend, what life may be?
Its green tongues whispered: Fates are three,
Life, my lad, is a dream of dree.

I said to the rocks—Can you tell me
Whether life be a dream of dree?
Their echoes answered, mockingly,
A dream—a dream—a dream—a dre—

I climbed; the mountain air was free.
Tell me, O hills, can this thing be?
Their shadows pointed silently :
Mapped below was a dream of dree.

I asked the plains the same query.
They stretched away unansweringly.
The pun was grim, but I could see,
They made it *plain*—a dream of dree.

I went and spake to the sounding sea,
Its waves came on unendingly,
Each as the last, and all agree
The flow of life is a dream of dree.

I questioned the heavens—Immensity
Smiled down in tender pleasantry:
It makes us *blue*, but a dream of dree
Is life throughout infinity.

THE SYLVAN SINGERS.

SUGGESTED BY A PAINTING BY E. W. MC DOWELL.

'TIS through the sylvan glades of Arcady
A maid goes pacing, piping fitfully,
Or singing little wood-songs, two or thee,

Anent the reeds and myrtles, red-rose-blooms,
The laurel glosses and the cypress glooms,
The shifting sunlight which them all illumes.

A maiden tall, fair-formed, and bannered with
A silken flag of red-gold hair, like myth
Of Dian, or the maids of wood god kith.

At peace, akin with all the furtive throng
Of wild-wood things she dreams them not a wrong,
But prone upon the sward pipes them this song:—

MAID SONG.

O sweet the light on the mist-blue hill;
Sweet is the light on the laughing rill;
Clear on the rocks at the cavern door;
Warming the moss on the forest floor;
Pleasantly falling on nest and lair,
Soft through the stream on the cataract stair.

Sweet and soft and bright and clear,
Sweet is the light and the light is here.

(ECHO:

Sweet—soft—bright and clear,
Sweet—the light—the light is here!)

* * * * *

Then with a flash and flutter of bright wings,
A little bird himself before her flings,
And lifting up his throat thus blithly sings:

BIRD SONG.

Sweet, sweet, sweet—
  Light,
      Light,
           Light!
Lips of music,
Eyes so bright;
Sunshine hair,
Shoulders white;—
O lady we love you,
  We wood-friends all;

THE SYLVAN SINGERS.

   We flutter above you,
    We whistle and call !
   In your breast,
   There to nest,
   Would be sweet,
    Sweet,
    Sweet !
And the wood-blossoms leap from the prints of
 your feet,
And the winds fall asleep in the net of your hair,
And the dews never weep, but forget their despair
When you walk where the moonbeams with you
 are so fair,
    Fair,
    Fair !
  Clear, clear, clear is my voice !
  Hear, hear, hear me rejoice !

 Lady, we love you !
  Lady we love you !
   Lady we love you here !

   (ECHO :

Lady—love !
 Lady—love you !
  Lady, we love you here !)

THE WORLD.

Fashion, the world, society, to me
 These ever are as some brave board outspread,
Where men and women feign to feast, unfed;
Smiling and gay, yet holding in each eye
The piteous glare of hunger's agony.
Ah! this alone is death, and these the dead;
And yet men call it " life " pitying, instead,
The child-like soul that loves simplicity.

A padded pomp, chill state, a gaslight glare,
 The bitter-sweet and dust of discontent,
  Soul-hunger and a secret none dare broach—

These are thy wages, world, thy servants wear
 Upon their brows the stamp of manhood spent,
  Lost innocence, and haunting, vague reproach.

SOUL AND SOIL.

FAIR the flower,
　　But the roots are found
In the rot, the grave, the ground;
Its nutriment and need they draw
From the corpses which they gnaw.

So,
Ebb and flow
Beauty, power, life's sweet play,
Chaos, weakness, sin, decay—
Tips the balance either way,
Rules the hour.

ONE MORE SONG.

I WILL sing one more song,
　　Full of bold, bright music,
The music of him of the glad eyes, the quick step,
　　the brave brow, the laughing lips, the frank
　　look, the true word;
The music of the free man.

A song of daring thoughts, of high hopes, of fear-
　　less faith;
A song of youth;

Of lilac skies, flakes of gold, and sunrise over the purple hills;
A song of morning;
A song of children playing in the warm sand, spattering the water with bare feet;
A song of seals sporting in the surf, with soft, loving eyes, barking like dogs;
A song of bright peaks, thunder, and the long, quivering lightning;
A song of dark waves, racing with the west wind, beating the rocks with a white foam;
A song of sea gulls;
A song of brilliant courage;
A song of innocent love;
A song of red flowers;
A song of white birds against a blue sky;
A song of a rock in the great sea which is always the same,
Whether the waves waste themselves upon it,
Or foam at its feet;
Whether the ice arms it with glittering mail,
Or the sun blisters it with angry heat;
Whether the rain weeps over it,
Or blue skies smile lovingly;
Whether the birds scream hoarsely about it,
Or come to it for rest and protection;
It is always there,
Calm, strong, beautiful:—

"I am a rock, I have foundations, I believe in myself;
I stand alone, or I stand with you, but I stand steadfast;
I am not troubled, I do not change—trust me!"

www.ingramcontent.com/pod-product-compliance
Lightning Source LLC
Chambersburg PA
CBHW020106170426
43199CB00009B/424